# Baby Sign Language

# Baby Sign Language

Alison Mackonochie

## PaRragon

Bath · New York · Singapore · Hong Kong · Cologne · Delhi · Melbourne

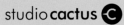

# Contents

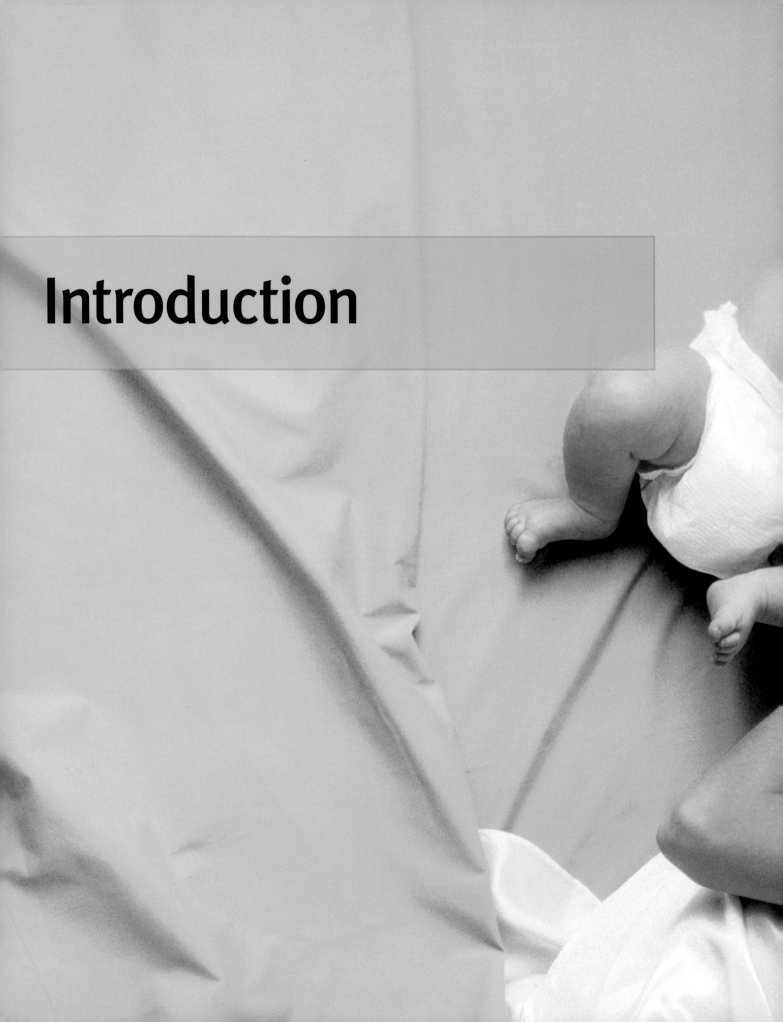

# Introduction

# WHAT IS BABY SIGNING?

Baby signing is a series of simple signs and gestures that allows your baby to communicate with you before he/she has developed the physical ability to coordinate the lip, tongue, and jaw movements needed for speech. It allows your baby to let you know what he/she feels or wants.

NATURAL ABILITY  We all use nonverbal communication techniques every day, and children quickly copy the ones they see adults using.

## UNIVERSAL LANGUAGE

Watch people talking together and you'll notice that we all do our own version of signing in conversations. Expressions and gestures help adults to communicate when there are language barriers to contend with, but, even among speakers of a shared language, we all use nonverbal communication

## "OFFICIAL" SIGNING

Sign Language has been used for many years as an effective form of communication for people who are hearing-challenged. This signing system is now recognized as a language in its own right and, just like any spoken language, it differs from country to country. The first

the official language for the deaf in the United Kingdom—while others, such as Makaton and Signalong, use some official sign language elements alongside other symbols, gestures, and words.

## Baby signs use everyday gestures —waving, pointing, nodding ...

techniques to help make ourselves understood. Some gestures are idiosyncratic but many are all but universal. Baby signs use many everyday gestures—waving, pointing, nodding—along with simple hand movements, to create a type of nonverbal "language."

baby signs were based on American Sign Language (ASL), but today other baby signing systems have been developed all around the world. Some of these use the official sign language of the country where they are used—for example, British Sign Language (BSL) is

## STAYING FLEXIBLE

The aim of this book, however, is not to teach your baby a new language, or to give you a set of specific signs that must be slavishly followed, but to give you the tools that will help your baby communicate before he/she can speak so that your child can connect more easily with you and others. These "tools" or signs can be adapted in any way that suits you and your baby. They have been chosen for their simplicity and their ease of use and are based on a mixture of "official" symbols and made-up signs. You can use them as they are portrayed, or simply as a basis for creating your own signs. The key is to stay flexible. Your baby may try to form a sign and consistently get it "wrong" but, as long as the sign remains consistent and you know what your baby is trying to say, that's fine. Go with your child's version.

**LOOK MOM, NO WORDS!** Whether you choose to use an official sign language such as ASL or make up your own signs, you'll be giving your baby a head start.

## HOW BABY SIGNING BEGAN

Dr. Joseph Garcia, an American child development expert, came up with the idea of teaching hearing babies sign language in the late 1980s. He'd seen how easily hearing babies of deaf parents learned sign language and had noticed how these babies were able to communicate long before they could speak. He did some research using ASL (American Sign Language) with babies of six and seven months, and found that by the time these babies reached eight and nine months they were able to communicate using the signs they'd been taught. This led him to develop his own system of sign language.

### ACREDOLO AND GOODWYN

At around the same time as Joseph Garcia was carrying out his research, Linda Acredolo and Susan Goodwyn—both American doctors—began to research a different style of baby signing. Rather than using ASL, they encouraged parents and babies to make up their own signs. Their study found that the parents of babies who had been taught to sign noticed that their babies appeared less frustrated because they could communicate more easily, and that this in turn strengthened the parent-child bond.

# THE BENEFITS OF BABY SIGNING

Undoubtedly, baby signing has many benefits both for babies and their parents. Signing helps you to recognize and satisfy your baby's needs, which in turn will lead to a happier baby. Being able to sign becomes especially helpful during the notorious "toddler years."

## HOT TOPIC

Baby signing classes sprang up first in the United States. Baby signing began to appear on TV programmes and in the press, which led to lively arguments over its benefits.

As recently as March 2007, a debate ("The Great Baby Sign Debate") concluded that although further research was needed to prove many of the longer-term benefits claimed by baby signing enthusiasts, such as a higher IQ and significantly greater and more rapid language and vocabulary development, there was no doubt about the beneficial value of the special interaction that occurs between parents and the babies who are taught to use signing skills.

TODDLER TANTRUMS
Toddlers are notorious for tantrums, which are often caused by their frustration at not being able to communicate what they want.

### WHY SIGN?

Babies who sign:
• are less frustrated
• are better able to communicate from an early age
• develop bigger vocabularies more quickly
• display an increased interest in books
• are more confident
• interact better with their carers
• may develop a higher IQ
• may start speaking earlier

## REAL BENEFITS

How does it help? Imagine that your nine-month-old baby wants a drink. You'd probably be able to discover this through a process of elimination, but the chances are that by the time you'd worked it out, your baby would be crying and you'd be stressed. Now imagine how much easier life would be if your child could just sign the word "drink." With baby signing skills, it is possible to do just that. And a little later, your baby can even specify what type of drink: milk or orange juice, for example.

## BONDING AID

Signing requires you to spend time on a one-to-one basis with your baby. Important interaction strategies are used during teaching, such as really focusing on things that interest your child, making eye contact, speaking slowly and clearly, and using simple words to describe what's going on around you.

Being able to sign will allow your child to take an active part in storytelling when you are looking at a book together. For example, when you look at pictures in a book with your baby, you naturally describe what's going on on each page. You may say something like: "Look at the ducks swimming on the pond." Once you have taught the signs for "duck" and "swimming," your baby will be able to join in the story.

## BOOSTING CONFIDENCE

Signing can be a useful way of interpreting your baby's first words, and can help you to understand the meaning of words that sound the same. Your baby may say "ca," which could mean "cat," "cake," or "car." If your baby can sign these words at the same time as saying them, it will help you to understand what is meant. And being able to make you understand will give your child the confidence to explore more words and signs and build a larger vocabulary.

One American study found that baby signers began to speak earlier than nonsigners and were more interested in books. When the children had reached the age of seven or eight years, it was discovered that they had a slightly higher IQ than the nonsigning group. Interesting though this study is, many professionals feel that before claims like this can be substantiated further research is required.

BABY BONDING Storytime with baby is a special bonding time for both of you—and a great time to practice signing.

# GETTING STARTED

Babies can sign as soon as they can control their hand movements, usually at around eight or nine months, although you can begin to teach your child the signs earlier than this. As for yourself, the good news is that you will already be familiar with much of the "new" language. Many of the physical gestures and expressions used in signing are a natural part of everyday conversations.

## WHEN SHOULD SIGNING BE INTRODUCED?

Although there are no hard and fast rules about when you should start signing with your baby, there are some facts that you may want to consider. Paradoxically, the earlier you start, the longer you may have to wait for your baby to start signing back to you. Six to eight months is often considered a good time to start teaching signs because a baby's memory retention increases rapidly from around this age. However, you will probably still have to wait for another couple of months before your baby begins to sign back.

The reason for the delayed reaction is quite simple; it is because if you introduce signing before your baby is physically and mentally ready to sign, he/she won't be *able* to respond. However, this doesn't necessarily mean that your baby isn't taking in the signs that you demonstrate—some babies who have been signed to from six months or even earlier seem to pick up new signs more quickly once they are old enough to sign themselves.

Do remember, though, that all babies are different: They develop at their own speed and there is nothing to be gained by trying to push them. Your baby will master signing when he/she is ready and not before, so keep it fun and don't get stressed about any lack of response. If signing stops being enjoyable, your

### ROUTINE

Don't imagine that teaching signing involves sitting down with your baby and introducing signs for a set period every day. Within a very short time you will both become very bored. It's much better to introduce signs as the words are used in day-to-day activities. By signing "cup" every time you pass your baby a cup, the action will help to associate the sign and the word and so help your child to learn the sign.

baby will have no interest in learning how to do it.

## WHICH SIGNS FIRST?

It doesn't really matter which signs you introduce first, but it makes sense to keep both the words and signs simple so that it is easier for your baby to pick them up. Don't overload a child with new signs. Choose four or five to begin with and keep using them in context even if you are getting no response from your child.

Introduce signs that your baby will find motivating. If you have started feeding solids and your baby isn't very interested, there will be no incentive for your child to learn the signs for "eat" or "more." However, teaching the sign for "milk" in this instance would give your baby a tool to ask for something that is really desired.

Signs for things that babies come across every day will be much more interesting to them than ones for items that have little or no part in their routine. For example, if you have a cat, your child will no doubt be fascinated by it, and may squeal with delight whenever it appears. You can use this interest to introduce a sign for "cat." This will be a lot more effective than teaching the sign for the cow you show your baby in a book. Gradually, once your baby has got the hang of signing, new words

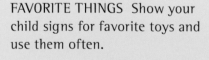

FAVORITE THINGS Show your child signs for favorite toys and use them often.

for things you come across in books or when you are out and about can be introduced, but in the beginning it's best to stay with familiar items.

## BE CONSISTENT

It's important to sign each time you use a chosen word so that your baby becomes familiar with both the sign and the sound of that word. For example, when your baby

needs changing you may say: "Is your diaper wet? Should I change you?" By signing "wet" and "change" each time, your child will quickly associate these signs with being changed. Although it may take a while for your baby to sign them back to you, once this milestone is passed your baby will be able to tell you when he/she needs changing. That's just another one of the many benefits of signing!

# SIGNING SKILLS

Although it is important not to become impatient if your baby doesn't seem to be picking up signing skills quickly —remember that all children will learn at their own natural pace—there are many techniques that you can use to help make signing easier for you both. These include simple ideas such as signing words for favorite activities— playing on the "swings" in the "park"—and more advanced methods for introducing signing sentences.

### FACE TO FACE

When you introduce a sign, it helps if your baby can see you clearly, so make sure you are face to face. Babies are naturally attracted to faces and will look toward your mouth when you speak, so once you have your baby's attention, sign close to your face. At this stage it's important to sign in context, so the association is clear. For example, if it is cold and your baby can feel the sensation of cold, he/she can make the connection between it being cold and the sign "cold." However, if you tell your baby that it is cold outside, but he/she is inside and warm, there is no connection to make.

FUN AND GAMES If you sit opposite, your baby can clearly see the signs you make. Keep your baby's attention by using favorite toys.

### AGAIN, AGAIN!

Repetition helps your baby make a connection between the object you are signing, the sign you are making, and the word you are saying. For example, whenever your pet dog comes into the room, you could sign and say "dog." Then go on to repeat the sign by introducing the word into conversation, saying things such as: "Can you see the dog?" "The dog is looking at you!" "I think the dog likes you!" If you need to catch your baby's attention, try putting some special emphasis on the word "dog," perhaps by using a different tone. If you do this every time your dog appears, your baby will gradually start to connect your family pet with the sign for dog and the sound of the word.

## MAKE IT A FAMILY AFFAIR

Once your baby has learned some signs, he/she will want to use them frequently, so there is no point in you both being the only people who understand what's going on. You'll need to involve your partner, siblings, grandparents, and babysitters, so that they too can take part in these non-verbal exchanges. You can

EXPRESS YOURSELF Where possible, use appropriate facial expressions to accompany signs, for example smiling when signing "happy" or frowning when signing "bad."

# It's important to sign in context so the association is clear.

teach adults in the same way as you've taught your baby, by introducing them to just a few signs at a time and using those signs whenever you use the words during conversations with your baby. Seeing them in action will help adults learn the signs more quickly. What's more, it's fun!

## WHEN YOUR BABY STARTS SIGNING BACK

It will take a while, but one day your baby will start signing back to you. You'll need to watch carefully so you don't miss these early signing attempts. They may not be too easy to recognize at first, but that's not important—the important thing is that your baby's signing. Give lots of praise and don't try to correct mistakes—just make sure that you keep signing correctly yourself. Over time the signs will gradually become more recognizable.

GOOD MANNERS Use playtime to teach signs for simple manners such as "please" and "thank you," "sorry" and "share."

your baby doesn't want to eat what you've chosen, or is bored with shopping and wants to go home!

## MAKING SENTENCES

Once your baby has built up a good signing vocabulary, you can start to put words together to make a signed sentence. These sentences will only be two or three words long, but they can convey a huge amount. For example, adding the sign for "more" to another sign, such as milk, you can ask if your baby wants "more milk." By putting "park," "swings," and "ducks" together, your baby can ask to go to the "park" to play on the "swings" and see the "ducks."

Being able to form a sentence is a big step in a child's development. To do this, your baby has to be able to think, understand, and communicate. Don't expect your child to grasp the idea of sentences right away: It will

You may find that once your baby has discovered the benefits of being able to communicate with you, he/she starts using other signs you've been using and is eager to learn more. Alternatively, you may have to wait for another week or even a month for another sign to materialize. Don't worry if there is a lull between the first and subsequent signs. This doesn't mean that your baby has gone off the idea or doesn't know any other signs: babies take things in at their own speed, which is fine.

This wonderful new form of communication doesn't always go according to plan—at least not the parent's plan, anyway. Once your baby has learned some signs, don't be surprised to find them used to his/her own advantage. For example, "finish" may be a sign you use to ask if your baby's finished something, or say that it's time to finish whatever you've been doing together. Having grasped the meaning, your baby may well use this sign to tell you when he/she has had enough. For example, you may find "finish" used to indicate that take time to understand what you are doing. Start with a couple of easy sentences and keep repeating them. You will probably get no response for some time, then suddenly your baby will catch on and sentences will become a normal part of conversation.

## SINGING AND SIGNING

Many nursery rhymes and songs for children are accompanied by gestures, so signing and songs go well together. Pick out two or three words to sign from a song and repeat these signs as you sing to your baby. For example, when you sing "Old MacDonald," you could make signs for each of the animals on the farm. While singing "Incy wincey spider," you could sign the words "spider," "rain," and "sun." Your baby will enjoy copying you, and will soon use these signs alongside any other gestures or noises the songs also require.

COMBINING SIGNS When beginning to practice sentences, try combining two simple words at first, such as "look" and "flower."

It's not just the playtimes and storytimes that offer opportunities for learning: All your daily routines—meal times, changing diapers, walks to shopping, bathtime, and bedtime—will be enriched by the introduction of signs and the thrill and satisfaction of seeing your baby communicate thoughts and feelings. Encourage your child to sign back to you by giving choices about activities. For example: "Do you want to go to the "park" or "shopping"?"

So, let's get signing. But remember, be patient; much as you want this dialogue to start, it does take time. Most importantly, keep it fun!

# First signs

# Everyday signs

Signing can seem like hard work in the beginning when you're getting little or no response from your baby. You can make it easier for yourself by starting off with a few simple signs for things that your baby is likely to use or do every day. Use the sign every time you use the word. This repetition will help you learn the signs along with your baby.

## FOOD FOR THOUGHT

Food plays a major part in your child's life—in fact, since birth your baby's world has centered around being fed. Most babies aren't very patient when they're hungry, either! That's why food is a good starting place for signing. Imagine your baby being able to tell you when he/she is hungry or thirsty, so that you can remedy the situation without any of the tears and tantrums caused because of the frustration of not being able to understand what your baby wants. Teaching your baby signs such as "milk," "drink," "cookie," and "more" will allow you to find out whether your baby wants to eat or drink, and will enable him/her to let you know when more milk or a cookie are wanted.

"Mommy" and "Daddy" are words your baby will have become familiar with at a very early age. Although there are recognized signs in every sign language for "Mommy" and "Daddy," you may like to develop your own. They could be something as simple as holding your hand palm down at eye level for "Mommy" and then doing the same action but with the hand held above the head for "Daddy." Whether you use existing signs or make up your own, do make sure that other people in your family are familiar with them, too. Consistency is very important if your baby is to understand the meaning of a sign.

## UNIVERSAL GESTURES

Of course, some everyday actions have universally accepted signs. Waving "goodbye" is one of the first gestures adults use to communicate with babies and this is often one of the first signs that babies learn to use themselves. Once waving has been mastered, it shouldn't be too long before your baby's on the way to signing words.

# drink and milk

Instead of having to second guess the reason for the crying, these signs will help you find out if your baby is thirsty and wants a drink, or would like some milk.

**DRINK** *Form a C shape using your whole hand. Bring the hand up to your mouth and make small tipping movements.*

**MILK** *Make your hand into a fist with the little finger nearest the floor. Now open and close your hand as though you are milking a cow.*

# eat and more

Meal times are social occasions that babies will enjoy, so pull the highchair up to the table and include your baby in your conversation.

**EAT** *Put your fingers and thumb together as though you're holding a piece of food, then tap them against your mouth several times.*

**MORE** *Bring your hands up in front of your chest, backs of fingers facing away from you, and touch the tips of the fingers of both hands together a few times.*

# cookie and cake

Whether you give them regularly or as a treat, cookies and cakes are always popular, so these signs should be favorites with your child.

**COOKIE** *Hold your right arm across your body with the palm facing down. Pinch together the fingers and thumb of your left hand and tap your right elbow twice.*

**CAKE** *Hold your right hand out flat with the palm facing up. Make a C shape using your left hand and with the fingers and thumb pointing down twist and raise this hand several times.*

# hello and goodbye

These gestures come naturally to adults and are easy for your child to pick up if you use them from a very early age. They are likely to be some of the first signs your baby makes.

**HELLO** *Hold your right hand level with your face with the palm facing forward and make a small waving motion from left to right.*

**GOODBYE** *With your hand held just above shoulder height and the palm facing forward, move your fingers down and up several times.*

# girl and boy

Children like to identify with others of the same gender as themselves and will quickly come to understand whether they are boys or girls.

**GIRL** *Hold your hand close to your face, palm facing forward and your index finger extended upward, then make small stroking movements against your cheek.*

**BOY** *Use your index finger and thumb to stroke both sides of your chin, bringing them together as though you are stroking a beard.*

# mommy and daddy

Your child will be familiar with these names from an early age. A version of "Mommy" and "Daddy"—perhaps "mama" and "dada" —are likely to be your baby's first words.

**MOMMY** *Using the first three fingers of your right hand, tap twice on the open palm of the left hand.*

**DADDY** *Form a C shape with your right hand and bounce it two or three times against the extended index finger of your left hand.*

# sister and brother

Signing siblings have a unique form of communication that will help them understand each other long before they have learned to speak.

**SISTER** *Bend the index finger of your right hand and tap it twice against your nose.*

**BROTHER** *Make both hands into fists and then rub them up and down against each other.*

# grandma and grandpa

Grandparents play a very special role in a child's life, so teaching your baby to sign their names will help to strengthen the bond there is between them. Both signs have two stages.

**GRANDMA** *Place your right fist on top of your left fist (main picture), then tap the first three fingers of your right hand on the open palm of the other hand to make the sign for "Mommy" (inset).*

**GRANDPA** *Place your right fist on top of your left fist (main picture), then make a C shape with your right hand and bounce it against the your left index finger to make the sign for "Daddy" (inset).*

# hot and cold

These are useful words to sign since you can use them as a warning against touching something dangerous as well as a description of how something may feel.

**HOT** *Hold your hand like a claw with the palm facing toward your mouth, then drop the clawed hand downward as if you are throwing something hot onto the floor.*

**COLD** *Place your closed hands in front of your body and pull your elbows into your sides as though you are shivering.*

# change and wet

Whether it's wet outside, or your baby has a wet diaper, this is a useful sign to know. And since being wet usually involves changing, this is another sign you'll find helpful.

**CHANGE** *Holding your two fists together, curled fingers touching but facing in different directions, pivot your hands in opposite directions.*

**WET** *Using one or both hands, close your fingers and thumb together several times.*

# careful and stop

These instructional signs can be very useful both around the home and when you are out and about. The "stop" sign can also be used for "hang on" and "wait."

**CAREFUL** *Make fists, then extend the first two fingers on each hand so that they look like scissors. Turn your hands sideways and tap one set of fingers against the other.*

**STOP** *Holding your hand up, palm facing outwards, make short pushing movements away from your body. You can add emphasis by using both hands.*

# help and hurt

It can be difficult to know whether a crying child is hurt or just frustrated. Teaching these signs will give your baby a way to communicate exactly what's wrong.

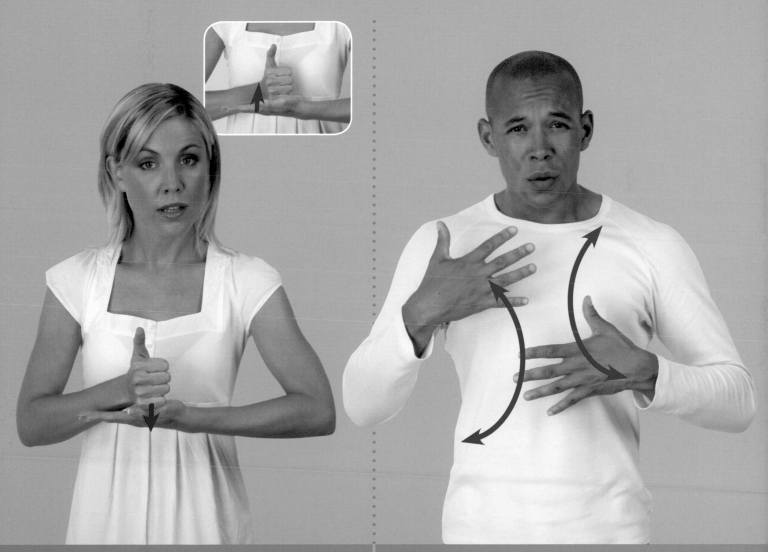

**HELP** *Rest your right fist on your left palm and move it forward for "I'll help you" (main picture) or back for "help me" (inset).*

**HURT** *With your hands flat, palms toward the body, shake them alternately up and down. You can indicate the hurt area by pointing with one hand while shaking the other.*

# come here and go

Being able to communicate these words
from a distance can be very useful,
especially when you are in a group
with other parents and their babies.

**COME HERE** *With your palm facing you
and your index finger extended, move the finger
backward and forward in a beckoning gesture.*

**GO** *Make fists, then extend the index fingers
and bend your hands at the wrist so that your
fingers are pointing in the direction you are going.*

# bed and sleep

Creating a relaxed bedtime routine will help your child settle more easily at night. This is a good time for a cuddle and a story before turning the lights out.

**BED** *Put one hand up to the side of your head and lean your head against it as though your head is on a pillow. This sign can also be used for "crib."*

**SLEEP** *With your palms together, hold your hands against the side of your head and then shut your eyes.*

# yes and no

Your child will probably already know how to nod for "yes" and shake the head for "no," but may enjoy using these signs as well for added emphasis.

**YES** *Make your hand into a fist with the closed fingers facing the floor and then move your wrist up and down as though your hand is nodding "yes." Nod your head at the same time for emphasis.*

**NO** *Cross your hands with the palms facing downward (inset), then uncross them swinging them sharply apart (main picture). Shake your head at the same time for more emphasis.*

# happy and sad

Learning about happy and sad feelings is an important part of a child's development. Use these signs to communicate that adults feel and understand the same emotions.

**HAPPY** *Place your hand flat against your chest and with a stroking movement repeatedly brush it up toward your neck.*

**SAD** *Using both your hands, hold them up in front of your face with your fingers spread so that you can see through them. Make a sad face as you draw your hands down to chest level.*

# At home

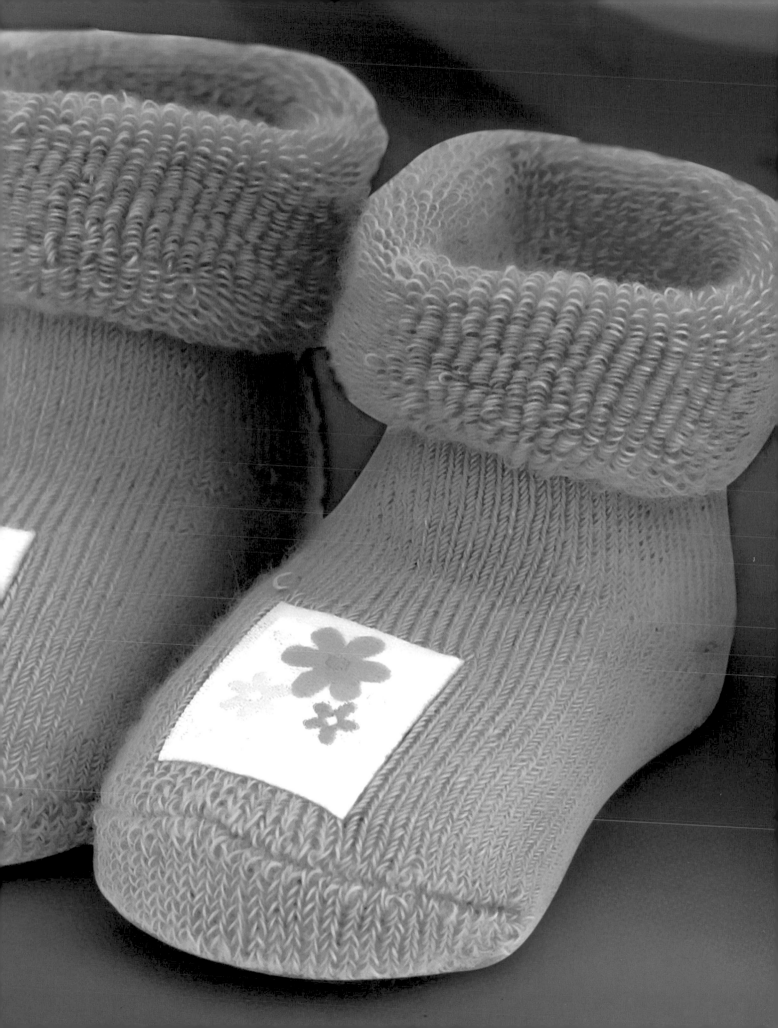

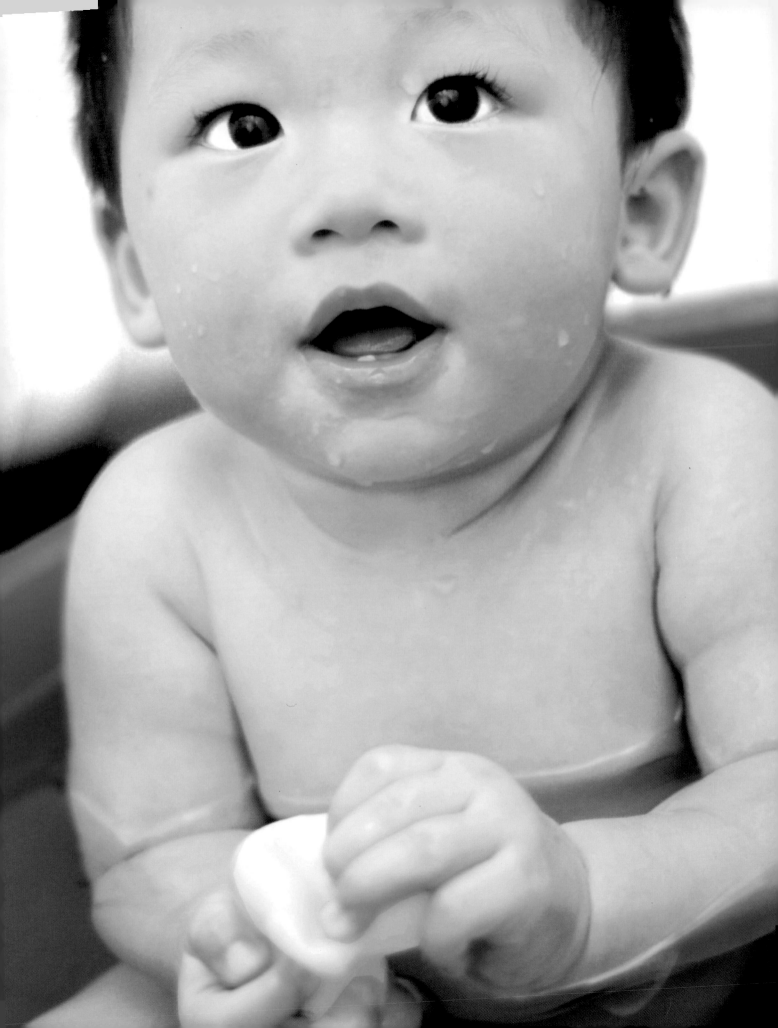

# Around the house

Daily routines, such as getting dressed or going to bed, are a great opportunity for signing. Try talking about the clothes you are putting on as you dress your baby, perhaps asking which pants you should choose today while you sign the word "pants," or suggest that your baby puts a coat on before you go out and sign the word "coat." If you sign words like these every day, your baby will soon become familiar with them.

## ADAPTING YOUR TECHNIQUE

It's not easy to hold a very young child's attention, so you will probably have to adapt your signing to fit in with whatever activity your baby's involved in. Rather than interrupting while your child's playing, try to incorporate signing into the play. For example, if your baby's playing with a favorite toy lamb, point to it and then sign the word "lamb." Remember to use the sign each time you talk to your baby about the lamb.

Some signs can be introduced by using your hands to "draw" them on your child's body. This lets your baby feel the sensation of the sign, which can be as effective as seeing it. For example, if your child is playing with the dog, you could tell him/her to be "gentle" by stroking your baby's forearm. Then you could show the sign for dog (see page 60) to link the two ideas.

## GIVE AND TAKE

Your baby will find passing an object between the two of you fun, and when you start signing it can help to keep your child's attention long enough to watch you sign the name of the item. Take something that interests your child, such as a feeding cup, and bring it toward you, signing the word as you do so, then pass it to your child. You will probably have long enough to show the sign before your baby's attention wanders. If you can get your child to pass the item back to you again, remember to sign as you take it. Make this into an enjoyable game and you'll be amazed how quickly your baby picks up the signs. Passing things backward and forward between you is also a good way of teaching the signs for "please" and "thank you" (see page 80).

# house and home

Although similar, these signs can be used to describe two different things. Your baby may use one of these signs for both words, but you'll soon notice the other clues.

**HOUSE** *Use your first two fingers to form an angle, then move them apart and down, making the shape of a building.*

**HOME** *With your hands flat, put your fingertips together to form a roof shape.*

# shoes and socks

It can often be a struggle to get your child to put socks and shoes on. Using signs to tell your child what you want him or her to do may help prevent arguments.

**SHOES** *Make two fists with your thumbs nearest to your body, then tap the sides of your fists together a few times.*

**SOCKS** *Extend the first two fingers on both hands and, putting both hands together, point the fingers toward your feet. Move them up and down alternately with your hands still touching.*

# coat and hat

Going outside can be an exciting adventure for your child, so talk about where you are going and what you might see as you put on your child's hat and coat.

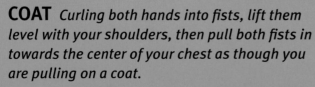

**COAT** *Curling both hands into fists, lift them level with your shoulders, then pull both fists in towards the center of your chest as though you are pulling on a coat.*

**HAT** *Holding your hand flat, pat the top of your head several times.*

# shirt and pants

Getting dressed in the morning doesn't have to be a chore. Talk about what each item of clothing is for as you put it on and your child will soon learn the routine.

**SHIRT** *With your index fingers and thumbs, pinch a bit of fabric from the shoulders of your shirt, and pull it upward and outward a few times.*

**PANTS** *Hold your hands at waist height with your fingers pointing downward, palms facing each other, then move both hands down one leg and then down the other.*

# brush and clothes

Make the most of the time you spend getting your child ready each day by talking about each of the activities, such as getting dressed, washing, and brushing hair.

**BRUSH** *Make your hand into a fist and then move it down beside your head as though you are brushing your hair.*

**CLOTHES** *With open hands, brush down your body using short repeated movements. You can also use this to mean "get dressed."*

# good and bad

Praise is important, so take every chance to let your child know that he/she has been good. There are also times when you need to tell your child that what he/she has done is bad.

**GOOD** *Make a fist and extend your thumb upward and then move the fist slightly up and down. For extra emphasis, use both hands. This can also be used as a sign for "hello."*

**BAD** *With your hand in a fist, extend the little finger and move it forward in short sharp movements. This sign can also be used to mean "naughty."*

# diaper and potty

If you can easily find out when your child is ready for a diaper change or needs to use the potty, it will save a lot of accidents, tears, and tantrums.

**DIAPER** *Hold your hands close to your body and snap your closed fingers against your thumbs.*

**POTTY** *Make your right hand into a fist and use your left index finger to make a horizontal circle above the fist.*

# kiss and cuddle

Kisses and cuddles are a natural part of your relationship with your baby, and they are especially important at bedtime since they will help to reassure and settle your child.

**KISS** *With the first two fingers on each hand extended, touch one set to your lips and then touch them to the other hand.*

**CUDDLE** *Cross your closed hands and with your shoulders raised, hug yourself as you twist your upper body slightly from side to side.*

# wash and dry

Your baby will enjoy getting messy and won't be so enthusiastic about being cleaned up. These signs are a useful way of indicating that playtime is over or bedtime is near.

**WASH** *Rub your hands together as though you are washing them. Use open hand movements around the face to indicate face washing.*

**DRY** *Rub your thumb backward and forward across the pads of your fingertips.*

# bath and towel

Water play at bathtime can be great fun, so "bath" could become one of your baby's favorite signs. You may both need a towel by the time you've finished all that splashing!

**BATH** *With your hands open and held flat against your chest, rub them up and down as though you are washing yourself.*

**TOWEL** *Hold one fist at shoulder height facing outward and one at waist height facing inward, then move them together diagonally as though you are drying your back with a towel.*

# down and sit

These two signs are especially useful because they can both be adapted to mean more than one word, but don't expect your baby to understand this immediately.

**DOWN** *Extend your index finger and, using a series of short moves, point down toward the floor. By reversing the position and pointing upward, you are making the sign for "up."*

**SIT** *Place your hands one on top of the other, fingers facing forward, then make short downward movements. Make short upward movements (hands still facing down) for "stand up."*

# family and baby

These are useful signs for describing your own family, and can be used when you are talking to your child about other people's families.

**FAMILY** *Extend the first two fingers of each hand and place one set of fingers over the other, then move them together in a small horizontal circle.*

**BABY** *Cradle one arm with the other and then rock them from side to side as though you are rocking a baby.*

# tv and telephone

Children often object to parents talking on the phone, so television can be a useful distraction. Some children's channels incorporate signing, so look out for these.

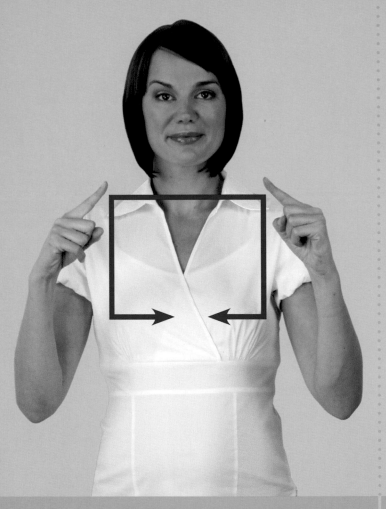

**TV** *Extend both your index fingers and use them to create a box in the shape of a television set.*

**TELEPHONE** *Extend your little finger and thumb and hold the other fingers against your palm, then raise the hand to your ear as though your hand was a telephone.*

# lie down and light off

Settling your baby at night isn't always easy, but being able to communicate that it's time to lie down and that you'll be turning the light off will help.

**LIE DOWN** *Use the index and middle finger on your left hand to form a V shape, then rest the V on your right palm (inset) and use it to make short movements to the left (main picture).*

**LIGHT OFF** *Hold your hand up level with your head with the fingers opened and pointing downward, or in the direction of the light, then snap them closed.*

# Out and about

# On the move

Once you and your baby have become used to signing at home, you can introduce signs for the things that you do and see when you are out together. The first signs you choose are likely to be dictated by where you live. If your baby sees cars, buses, and stores when you go out, then these are obviously the best signs to teach. However, if chickens, cows, and tractors are more familiar to your child, then signs for these will have more relevance.

## PUTTING WORDS TOGETHER

Each time you suggest to your child that you should go for a walk, remember to sign "walk." Children generally love being outside and enjoy the prospect of going for a walk to "go shopping" or to the "park," two more popular signs you can introduce. Wherever you live, signs for "flower" and "tree," "walk" and "stroller" will have their place in your child's signing vocabulary. Similarly, there will always be opportunities to point out animals. It's worth learning individual signs for common pets such as dogs and cats that you will see regularly, but you can also learn the more general sign for "animal" for those exciting moments when you catch a glimpse of a wild creature such as a squirrel. Use opportunities to repeat a sign; for example, if you see three ducks, sign "duck" three times.

Once you've introduced a few signs, you can start putting them together, so for example you could say: "Shall we put you in your "stroller" and "walk" to the "park" to feed the "ducks?" "

## WEATHERWISE

As adults we often think it's boring to talk about the weather, but it's a great topic for signing. If it's hot outside, you will want to put sunscreen on your baby. Signing "sun" and "hot" (see page 30) will help your baby understand the need to have cream on. The same goes for "rain" and having to wear a "coat" (see page 44). Your baby will be most interested in things that are being seen and experienced. Signing "wind" when you are both outside and can feel the breeze will make a lot more sense to your child than signing "wind" when no wind can be seen or felt.

# dog and cat

Animals hold a special fascination for young children—just take a look at your child's face when seeing a cat or meeting a friendly dog in the park!

**DOG** *Holding your hands in front of you with index and middle fingers extended, like a dog in a begging position, make small repeated downward movements.*

**CAT** *Flexing your fingers slightly, move your hands out from the sides of your mouth across your cheeks to indicate whiskers. Repeat several times.*

# duck and bird

Some really simple activities often give the greatest pleasure, and your child will soon be able to tell you clearly that he/she wants to go to the park to see the ducks.

**DUCK** *With your hand held near your mouth, open and close your fingers against your thumb as though you are imitating a duck's bill.*

**BIRD** *With your hands in made into fists, bend your arms in at the elbows and move them up and down as though you are flapping wings.*

# animal and park

A trip to the local park can be the highlight of your baby's day, not only because of the swings and seesaws but also because of the opportunity to spot local wildlife.

**ANIMAL** *With hands held like claws pointing toward your chest, make clawing movements in little forward circles alternately, moving up and down as though scratching at your chest.*

**PARK** *Hold your hand flat and at an angle with the index finger nearest you, then tap the hand twice against your upper chest.*

# flower and tree

Even in a city you will be able to point out trees and flowers to your child. You can encourage an interest in nature by teaching these signs.

**FLOWER** *With your fingers flat against your thumb, place them to the right of your nose and then move the hand in an arc until it reaches the left side of your nose, as though smelling a flower.*

**TREE** *Rest your right elbow on your left hand. Spread the fingers on your right hand and make repeated twisting movements from the wrist, like a tree blowing in the wind.*

# horse and sheep

These animals are firm favorites with children and are often to be found as characters in children's programs on television and in storybooks.

**HORSE** *Hold your hands in front of you as if you are holding the reins of a horse and make short repeated movements forward and down.*

**SHEEP** *Use your extended little fingers to make small circular movements near the side of the head as though indicating ram's horns.*

# wait and look

These two signs are especially useful when it comes to explaining road safety. Use them every time you cross the road, so that your child becomes familiar with them.

**WAIT** *With hands bent, fingers toward the ground, make two short downward movements.*

**LOOK** *Use your middle and index fingers to form a V and point them toward your eyes (main picture). Use the V shape to point if you want to indicate a specific object (inset).*

# run and hurry

Getting children to hurry isn't always easy, so being able to use signs to emphasize the fact that you need your child to move along may help to speed up the process.

**RUN** *Move your fists backward and forward alternately at the side of your body as though you are running.*

**HURRY** *Extend the index fingers on both hands and then repeatedly bounce the right finger sharply against the left.*

# how many? and where?

These are great signs for you to use when your child is old enough to enjoy playing simple games and is beginning to learn about numbers.

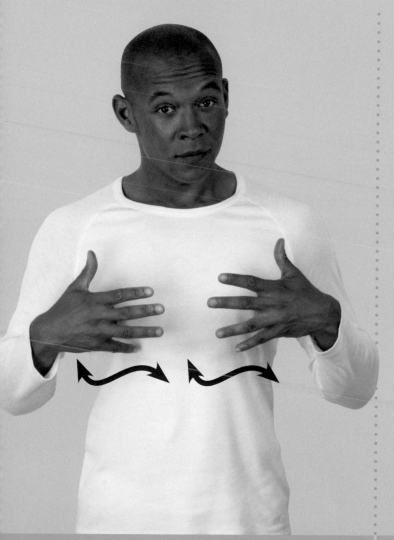

**HOW MANY?** *Raise your eyebrows and with your hands flat, palms toward your body, wriggle your fingers as your move your hands apart.*

**WHERE?** *Hold your hands out flat in front of you, palms upward, and move them in small outward circles. Raise your eyebrows to emphasize the question.*

# noisy and quiet

When you're out and about you might want to mention the noise of a busy city street. Or you may need to tell your child to be quiet if you visit a place where noise is inappropriate.

**NOISY** *Use your index finger to point at your ear while rotating the finger in small forward circular movements.*

**QUIET** *Hold your index finger to your lips (main picture), then, using the thumbs and index fingers on both hands to form an O with the palms facing forward, move the hands slowly apart (inset).*

# moon and night

These signs go hand-in-hand and are very useful when it comes to bedtime. The moon often features in nursery rhymes and stories, too.

**MOON** *Make a C shape with one hand and place it close to your eye. Keeping the shape, move your hand up and follow it with your eyes so that it looks as though you're looking at the moon.*

**NIGHT** *With your hands facing toward you, swing them in and down so that they cross each other. This sign also means "dark." Reverse it to make the sign for "day" or "light."*

# plane and train

These are particularly fascinating to children because one flies in the air like a bird, while the other whooshes past at high speed. The noise they make can be loud and thrilling.

**PLANE** *Extend your thumb and little finger to form a Y shape and then, with your hand at head height, move it forward and up and down like a plane bobbing up and down in flight.*

**TRAIN** *Make your hand into a fist and then move it in small circles at the side of your body, like the wheels of a train.*

# bus and car

Whether you travel by car or bus, go for walks and see traffic on the roads, or just play with a model car, your child will be interested in all the vehicles he/she sees.

**BUS** *With your hands placed fairly wide apart, close your fists with the palms upward and make small backward and forward movements as though steering a large vehicle.*

**CAR** *With your hands quite close together, make them into fists as though you are holding a steering wheel. Then move your hands up and down as you would when driving.*

# stroller and walk

Going for a regular walk with your baby is not only good exercise for you, but a great way of introducing your child to the world outside the home.

**STROLLER** *Hold your hands as though you are gripping the handle of a stroller and then make forward pushing movements.*

**WALK** *Use the index and middle finger of your right hand to make walking movements across the palm of your left hand.*

# wind and rain

Your baby will enjoy "conversations" about the weather, especially when the effects of wind blowing the trees and rain splashing on puddles can be seen.

**WIND** *Extend your arms in front of your body with your palms facing, then move them from side to side as though they are being blown by the wind.*

**RAIN** *With your hands open and palms facing toward the floor, make repeated downward movements in front of your body.*

# sand and sun

Those first trips to the beach are always special. Sand is endlessly fascinating for children, and sunshine is always welcome (don't forget baby's hat and sunscreen).

**SAND** *With your fingers pointing toward the floor, hold your hands at waist height and rub your thumbs across your fingertips as if you're letting sand run through them.*

**SUN** *Hold your hand above your head, palm downward, with your fingers spread to represent the sun's rays.*

# road **and** store

Stores are fascinating places to your baby, so build up the anticipation by describing where you're going, the trip, and what you're going to see when you get there.

**ROAD** *Hold your hands out flat, palms facing and fingers pointing down (main picture), then bring the hands up until they are pointing forward (inset).*

**STORE** *With your hands at chest height, fingers pointing toward the ground, make two short downward movements.*

# Playtime

# Learning is fun

Play isn't just about having fun and bonding with your child, it's also important for your baby's development. It will help with hand/eye coordination and encourage your baby's skill at manipulating objects, while also teaching about cause and effect. As play becomes more creative, your baby will learn self-awareness and imagination. Naturally you'll want to help and encourage your baby and here signing can be of great benefit to you both.

## IMAGINATIVE PLAY

Signing will help your child to tell you about his/her play. For example, your child may be putting toy animals in a box. All you can see is toys and a box, but in your baby's imagination it's horses going into a stable in a farmyard, just like the one you saw on your walk yesterday. If your baby is able to sign the word "farm" and "horses" (see page 64), you will soon be able to work out the rest of the story.

Singing and signing can be fun, too. Adding a few signs to nursery rhymes will encourage your child to join in when you sing. For example, "Mary had a little lamb, its fleece was white as snow" can become a signing song by adding signs for "lamb," "white," and "snow." Substitute your child's name for "Mary" for added interest. Think of the fun you can have with Old MacDonald and his farm—not only making animal noises, but also introducing signs for each of the animals on the farm. Don't be afraid to make up new signs, as long as you and your family members use them consistently.

## SIMPLE MANNERS

Playtime is a good time to teach simple manners, so introduce signs for "please" and "thank you," "you," "me," and "sorry" now, since you'll have plenty of opportunity to use them when you take turns during a game.

You will no doubt say "I love you" to your child many times in a day, but you can sign it too, and, most importantly, once the sign is mastered, your baby will be able to tell you that he/she loves you, too. The first time your baby signs it back will be a truly magical moment. Happy signing!

# please and thank you

If you use and sign these words from an early age, it will encourage your child to use them naturally once he or she learns to speak.

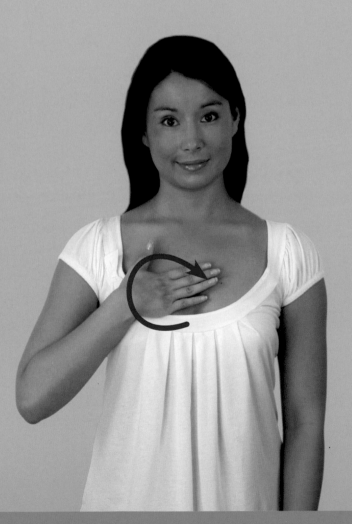

**PLEASE** *Place your hand flat against your chest then make a circle, repeating as necessary for emphasis.*

**THANK YOU** *Touch your chin with your fingertips (main picture), then let the hand drop forward with the palm facing upward (inset).*

# I love you

Three little words that sum up everything you feel about your child. Imagine the thrill when your child can sign them back to you! There are two simple versions of this sign.

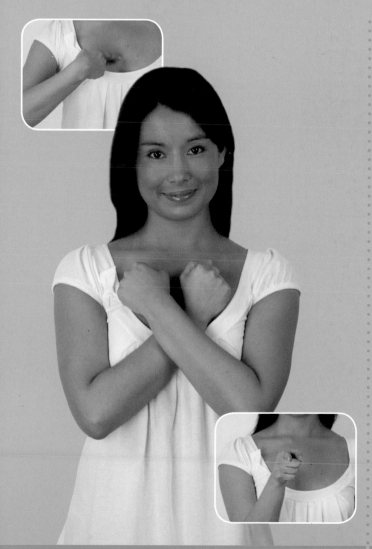

**I** *Use your index finger to point at yourself (top inset).*
**LOVE** *Make your hands into fists and cross them over your chest at the wrists (main picture).*
**YOU** *Point at the other person (bottom inset).*

**I LOVE YOU** *Hold up your right hand, facing outward, and raise your index and little fingers upward and extend your thumb.*

# play and share

Play helps a child's physical and social development. Learning to share during play can be difficult for your child. Using the "share" sign can act as a gentle reminder.

**PLAY** *Hold your hands, palms upward, in front of you, and then, using upward movements, circle them simultaneously.*

**SHARE** *Place the edge of one hand on the open palm of the other and rock it from one side to the other.*

# book and story

It's never too soon to introduce your baby to books. From a very early age, a child will enjoy sitting with you and looking at pictures while you read the story.

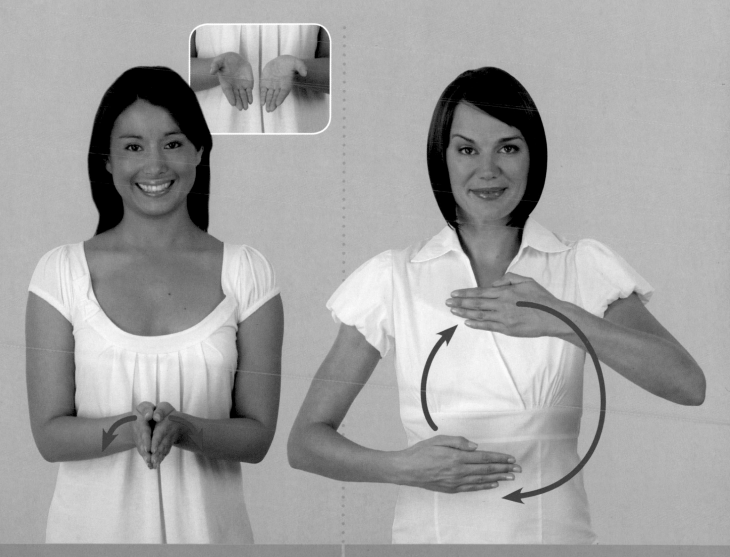

**BOOK** *Hold your hands together, palms facing (main picture), and then open them out like a book (inset).*

**STORY** *Put one hand on top of the other with the palms facing toward you, then rotate them in a forward circular movement. This sign also means "explain" and "tell."*

# swing and slide

A trip to the park often means playtime on the swings and slide, which can be very exciting. The sign for slide is usually followed by "more" and "more."

**SWING** *Make your hands into fists and, holding them in front of you, make several forward (main picture) and backward (inset) swinging movements.*

**SLIDE** *Hold one hand open, palm up, extend and bend the first two fingers of the other hand (inset), then slide these fingers down the length of the open hand as though they are on a slide (main picture).*

# swim and water

Baby swimming classes are great fun and a good way for parents to spend quality time with their children. You'll be amazed how quickly your child becomes a water baby!

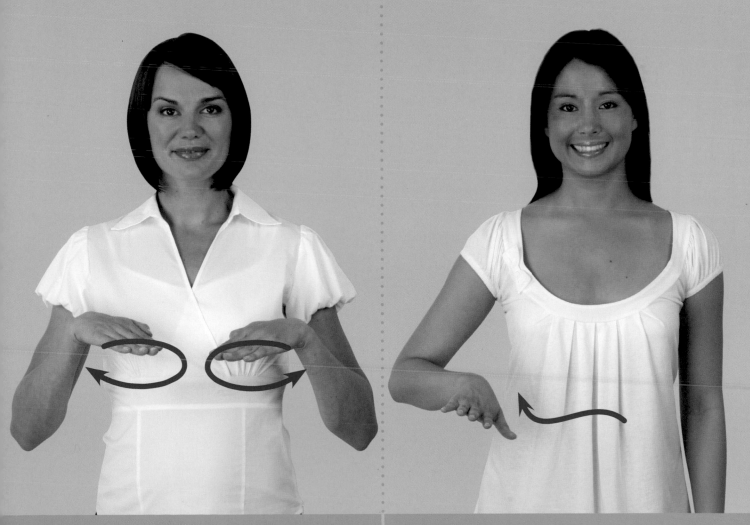

**SWIM** *Hold your hands flat in front of you with the palms down and move them in small outward circles as though you are pretending to do the breast stroke.*

**WATER** *With your hand flat and palm facing downward, make small wavy movements as your hand moves to the right. To indicate a drink of water, brush your throat repeatedly with your bent hand.*

# toys and doll

Toys are great learning tools for young children and your child will no doubt have some firm favorites that are played with more than others.

**TOYS** *Hold your right hand out flat and use your left hand to form a T shape, then move both hands together in a small inward circle.*

**DOLL** *Rest one hand on top of the other and move them from side to side in a small rocking motion.*

# ball and bike

Outdoor play gives your child the fresh air and exercise needed to be healthy. Learning to ride a bike and playing ball are good ways to start.

**BALL** *Form a C shape with each hand and, with the fingers spread, bounce the hands toward each other until they touch, forming the shape of a ball.*

**BIKE** *Make two fists and, holding them in front of your body, rotate them as though they were the pedals on a bike.*

# friend and comforter

Friendships with other children take time to develop, but from an early age your child is likely to have a toy or a cuddly blanket that is used as a comforter.

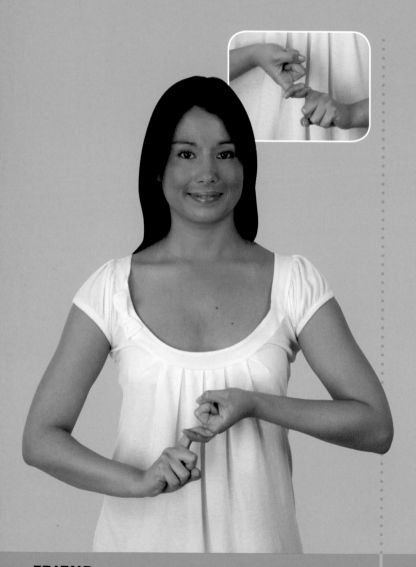

**FRIEND** *Lock your index fingers together (main picture) then change positions and lock them the other way (inset).*

**COMFORTER** *Cross your arms over your chest with your palms up near your shoulders, and rub your upper chest with your fingertips a couple of times.*

# finish and tidy up

Being able to indicate in advance that play is coming to an end and that toys need to be tidied away will help to prepare your child and avoid tears of disappointment.

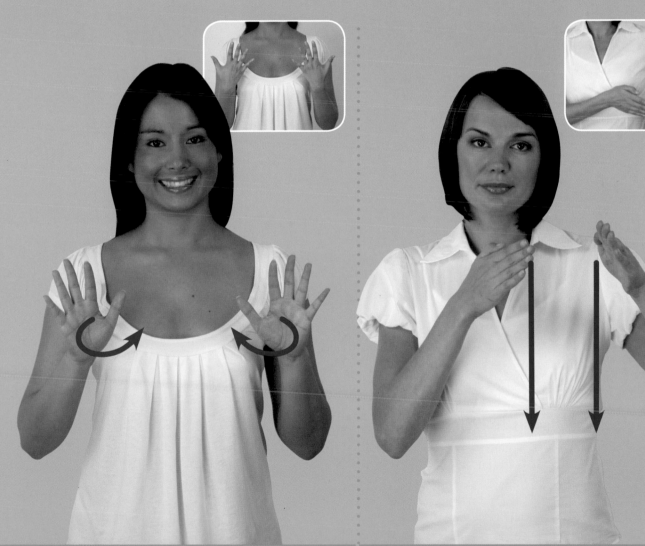

**FINISH** *Hold both hands up near your shoulders with the palms facing forward (main picture), then rotate your hands at the wrists so that the palms face the body (inset). Repeat several times.*

**TIDY UP** *With your hands flat and facing each other at shoulder height (main picture), make short downward movements first to the left side (inset) and then to the right.*

# sorry and you/me

Games will be a lot more fun once your child understands about having to take turns and knows how to indicate when he or she has made a mistake.

**SORRY** *Curl one hand into a claw shape, lift your shoulders, and shake the hand back and forth at the side of the head (main picture). Alternatively, use a fist to make small circles on your upper chest (inset).*

**YOU/ME** *For "you," use your index finger to make small jabbing movements as you point at the other person (main picture). Point at yourself in the same way for "me" (inset).*

# laugh and cry

Laughter and tears are a normal part of every child's life. Being able to sign that you understand such feelings will increase your child's confidence.

**LAUGH** *Place the tips of your index fingers at the corners of your mouth (inset) and draw them outward into a smile, remembering to smile as you do so (main picture). Repeat several times.*

**CRY** *Using the index fingers on both hands, brush them alternately down your cheeks several times to indicate tears falling.*

# time and what?

These two signs can greatly enhance your "conversations" since they allow you to ask questions of each other and help you to indicate that it's "time" to do something.

**TIME** *Using your right index finger, tap the back of your left wrist twice.*

**WHAT?** *With your hand at shoulder height, the palm facing forward, extend your index finger and shake it from side to side in short quick movements. Make sure your expression is quizzical.*

# which? and who?

Giving your child the means to ask questions rather than just naming objects will open up a whole new dimension to your nonverbal conversations.

**WHICH?** *Make your hand into a fist, then extend the little finger and thumb and make small side-to-side movements. Use your expression to reinforce the question.*

**WHO?** *With the palm facing left, use the index finger on your right hand to tap your chin twice, with an inquiring expression on your face.*

# INDEX   References in **bold** refer to signs

"bed"

"telephone"

# ACKNOWLEDGMENTS

**Alison Mackonochie** would like to thank Ann Edwards 'Granny Annie', and Vikki and Ella McIntyre for sharing their signing experiences with me. Special thanks, too, to Robin for always being there when I need him.

**Studio Cactus** would like to thank BMA Model Agency, Anna de Kretser for make-up, and the models used in this book: Joanne Batten, Emma Cooper, Lucy Piper, and Chris Timony.

The publishers would like to thank the following for permission to reproduce copyright material:

Abbreviations: a = above, b = below, l = left, r = right, t = top

PhotoDisc, p 90 (tr), pp 6–7; Photos.com, p 35 (t); aaah, p 91 (tl); AGphotographer, p 78; Alexander Motrenko, p 44 (t); Alison Williams, p 37 (tr); Andresr, p 49 (t); Andy Lim, p 40; Anita Patterson Peppers, p 55 (t); Antonio Jorge Nunes, p 63 (t); APSchorr, p 43 (t); Boleslaw Kubica, pp 76–77; Brian McEntire, p 52 (t); Charlene Bayerle, p 64 (tl); Chris Sargent, p 62 (t); Craig Barhorst, p 71 (ta); dainis, p 48 (t); Daniel Gale, p 80 (t); Darren Baker, p 26 (t); Dee Hunter, p 91 (tr); digitalskillet, p 27 (t), p 53 (t); dwphotos, pp 56–57; Eimantas Buzas, p 58; Ekaterina Monakhova, p 28 (t); EML, p 87 (tr); Franz Pfluegl, p 13; Fred Goldstein, p 66 (t); Gary Sludden, p 46 (t); George Allen Penton, p 67 (tl); Goh Siak Hian, p 8 ; Gravicapa, p 87 (tl); iofoto, p 68 (t); Iurii Konoval, p 70 (tr); javarman, p 64 (tr); Johanna Goodyear, pp 18–19; Juriah Mosin, p 24 (t), p 84 (t5), p 90 (tl); Karen Roach, p 25 (t); Katharina Wittfeld, p 82 (t); Katrina Brown, p 10; Kristian Sekulic, p 34 (t); Lane V. Erickson, p 69 (t); Leah-Anne Thompson, p 33 (t); Lenets Sergey, p 92 (t); Lisa F. Young, p 32 (t): Losevsky Pavel, p 75 (t), p 83 (t); Lowell Sannes, p 74 (t); Magdalena Szachowska, p 86 (t), p 89 (t); Natalia V Guseva, pp 38–39; Niamh Baldock, p 54 (t); Obivan, p 22 (t); OlgaLis, p 67 (tr); Otmar Smit, p 61 (t); Patrick Breig, p 71 (tb); Pavel Pospisil, p 84 (tl); PeterG, p 20; Rene Jansa, p 14; rickt, p 45 (t); Robert Cumming, p 93 (t); Robynrg, p 42 (t); Shutterstock, p 37 (tl); sierpniowka, p 31 (t); signorina, p 30 (tl); Simone van den Berg, p 88 (t); Sonja Foos, p 73 (t); Stas Volik, p 85 (t); Stephen Finn, p 65 (t); Stephen Strathdee, p 70 (tl); Stiggy Photo, p 30 (tr); Stuart Monk, p 29 (t); Supri Suharjoto, p 47 (t); Tina Rencelj, p 60 (t); Tiplyashin Anatoly, p 72 (t); Tjerrie Smit, p 50 (t); Tomasz Trojanowski, p 36 (t), p11; Viktoriya, p 51 (t); Vivid Pixels, p 23 (t); Zsolt Nyulaszi, p 16, p 17, p 81 (t)

All other images © Studio Cactus